TØ167508

ONE, TWO

Angela Leighton was born in Wakefield, educated in Edinburgh and Oxford, and has taught at the universities of Hull and Cambridge. The daughter of a Yorkshire father and a Neapolitan mother, she has always recognised her heritage of mixed languages and conflicting assumptions. Perhaps for this reason her work has always pushed at the boundaries of literary form. Her most recent critical book, *Hearing Things: The Work of Sound in Literature* (2018), sets creative prose alongside critical thinking to suggest the connections between them. She has published short stories and reviews in many journals, as well as four previous volumes of poetry: *A Cold Spell* (2000), *Sea Level* (2007), *The Messages* (2012) and *Spills* (2016) – this last interweaving memoir, short story, translation (from the Italian) as well as original poetry.

Poetry

Spills (Carcanet, 2016)
The Messages (Shoestring, 2012)
Sea Level (Shoestring, 2007)
A Cold Spell (Shoestring, 2000)

Critical

Hearing Things: The Work of Sound in Literature (Harvard, 2018)
Voyages over Voices: Critical Essays on Anne Stevenson (ed) (Liverpool, 2010)
On Form: Poetry, Aestheticism and the Legacy of a Word (Oxford, 2007)
Victorian Women Poets: Writing Against the Heart (Harvester, 1992; 2019)
Elizabeth Barrett Browning (Harvester, 1986)
Shelley and the Sublime (Cambridge, 1984; 2013)

One, Two

ANGELA LEIGHTON

CARCANET

First published in Great Britain in 2021 by
Carcanet
Alliance House, 30 Cross Street
Manchester M2 7AQ
www.carcanet.co.uk

A CIP catalogue record for this book is
available from the British Library.

ISBN 978 1 800170 16 2

Book design by Andrew Latimer
Printed in Great Britain by SRP Ltd, Exeter, Devon

The publisher acknowledges financial
assistance from Arts Council England.

For Harriet, as ever, walking on

CONTENTS

'I'll sing you one, O.'
– 'Green Grow the Rushes, O'

'I must have two, *you know… One to come, and one to go.'*
– Lewis Carroll

'See, they return; ah, see the tentative
  Movements, and the slow feet.'
– Ezra Pound

SEA SONG

Sewer and salve, dredge and dump, kitten and killer,
sea, our element, lovely other, soul and matter,
intricate jeweller of caves and corals, molluscs and pearls,
salty original, mirror of weather, flood of tears.

Sea, our crossing, launch and offing, lift and tease,
as if a loop of dolphins took us, deeper to breathe,
darker to see, further to hear – from dream to after,
through flesh, fish, shell, krill, to the first life-matter.

ISLAND / POEM

Think – an island interests the poem.
Each grounded tally pegs the drift,
snags a silkie from the liquid swell
   where grey beasts swim.

What's missed still calls from roke and fret.
Sing-song of shorelines scores each edge
where sea will pocket stones for the sea-bed,
   and nothing lies still.

Consider – an island interests the poem.
Each shape amended to a perfect cone
caps the slick of what's not known,
   but whispers below.

STORMY PETREL

Turquoise, azure, indigo, blue –
and below, the opal of a perfect pearl
pools all colours to a translucent whorl.

I cannot enter that abstraction of despair,
the witch's mirror in which we disappear
to breathe blue water, choke on the sea's tear.

I cannot know how one word – *celeste* –
might yet transpose to liquid syllables below,
and sound a glass bell in that deafening hollow.

So I watch this small bird that patters with its feet
the thin line Peter could not walk for drowning.
Fisher of small fry, it flip-flops, grounding

the vast sea-level's intemperate upheavals.
Tiny, sparrow-sized, flutter-running thing –
on the sea's blue page, the superscript of a wing.

BARN OWL

Winging hard by,
sheer and level, quick and killing –
Barn Owl, Billy Wix, Ginny Ollit –
a plectrum of feathers taps the quiet,
riffs the static of a summer night.

Parrying a fall
with tucked claws, balancing wings,
its hunched drag quartering the moorlands,
feather finials hallucinating hands –
what ghost inhabits this fanning thing?

Steering too close
to us, then clear, past omens, scares –
we stand, queer giants, at the dark's address,
no interruption of its watchfulness –
this fly-by-night fingering the air.

Idling so near
it shames us, casts us into shadow –
while a drifted whiteness comes to mind,
wing of the moon, or whitsun crosswind
brushing lightly – claw at a heartstring.

HUMMING-BIRD HAWK-MOTH

Late in a garden I turn each page.
The day's evening waits in the wings –
old words singing by heart almost
till I reach that roll-call in parenthesis:
(*Enter Pease-blossome, Cobweb, Moth*).

How reading dreams its own known story:
a summer love tale, *the tongs and the bones*,
till all turns fairy, lifts and stirs
in lighter repeats, in tactical-heard
flights *between the cold moon and the earth*.

Then something throws its counterweight –
this furry mimic of a rotary blade,
micro-flyer that darts and stays
at any summered jasmine, woodbine –
one flute filament tippling its new wine.

And fifty-wingbeats-per-second drives
that motor levity, the fret of a hum –
migrant stranger in a blur of wings
magicked from a call long-lost, unplayed:
'(*Enter... Moth*)' – but for what? No word –

unless just to cue a wandering soul,
a creature answering to some lost part,
– like this mere moth, a thing that lives.
So nature's intricate knack of the ordinary
outwits those marvellous plots of names.

STEP CHANGE

Beside the compost's vegetable waste
juiced to a wormy, sun-proved manure,

it seemed an angel feathered into stone,
flat-packed to earth in a fringe of wings,

stubbed to a level, weathered to no name
and grey from rinsing under days of rain.

Now, there's only a faintness stamped,
reverse transcendence assuming its blank

where once the stencil of a hapless bird
chalked the pathway like a hopscotch turn –

mere sketch of bones in a tent of skin,
the living flight left blazoned in.

Yet still, the touching palms of my feet
sidestep an angel skies can't delete.

SAVING HIS GLOVES
for Marion

I count five fingers to a dead mole's hands –
scullers, big shovellers, flat on the hillside,
pink and raw beside a wrap of moleskin,
manuals, movers – like something human
coming to light under the sun.

Small blind miner with the capable hands
that once moved mountains, inch by inch,
earth-shifter, mouldwarp, now cold aboveground,
morkin dumped among your nunkey tumps,
old mole, ghosted into two small gloves.

And I remember others, the ones she saved…
old suede, knuckled by years of wear,
close as houses, yet moulded, stretched
over the stored hold of an absence –
light touch, answering hand to hand.

She'll slip them on sometimes and feel
their give, their easy accommodation,
push her fingers to the limits to know
(in the found art of a lost thing)
his nowhere reaches, stranger bearings.

MY DOG OSCAR

after Christopher Smart & A.E. Stallings

For I will consider my dog Oscar.

For he does not consider verse a fit or fortunate activity,
                    but grieves for the time wasted, the delay,

and drums his tail for a sign, and sighs, a canicular lament
                    for the hours passing, the best moment missed.

For he can run for sheer joy of the wind, when wind is a tease and a
                    torment, making his thick fur stare.

For he was born under the sign of Sirius, brightest of stars,
                    and he can catch any twinkle in an eye.

For he will die under the sign of Cerberus, grimmest of wards,
                    guarding the way of no return.

For there is no unearthly yen about him, no ever-shall-be
                    that is not now, or here, or this,

no elsewhere ghosting the good stench of things, no dybbuk gibbering
                    in the fat substance of perceivable facts.

For he goes nose to the moment, stepwise, footing it slick,
                    4.4 at a trot, 2.2 bounding.

For he greets nothing that is not there in the nostrils' sensing,
                    in the audio-ambry of his periscope ears.

For he can make prosody out of a run, muscling in on
                    earth's hard base, air's pure give,

phrasing the way of it, extemporising dynamics of a praise-song
                    for all creation laid at his feet.

For he is dog's-body and all the naturalised mongrels are his:
                    dog-rose, dog whelk, dogwood, doggerel,

all the crossed, irregular castes, the polymorphed forms
                    of life's endlessly evolving bounty.

For he will piss openly on upstanding things, respecting no status,
                    but furiously back-kick the steam of his shit.

For his is the law of the instant, he trails any stink or rustle,
                    obeys the command of stomach and bowel.

For he will growl through his teeth, feeding, wolfing dog's dinners
                    like the last bones filched in prehistory.

For his fur hackles at a forest call: for beasts in a pack,
                    moons that cue longing and howling.

For he can dig deep, snuffing the soul that's folded round bone –
                    quick forensics for an Anubis –

or nuzzle to speak, intelligencing the uncrossable sea
                    that keeps us, creature-continents, apart.

For scenting a bitch on heat he will dash, abandoning me utterly,
                    bent on pleasure fit to break my heart.

For spent, he will return with a dog-look sorrowed by all love's puzzling,
                    chase and satiety, impulse and expense.

For his paws are pillowed and palmy between claws, handy on all-fours,
                    tough as old boots on a rocky foreshore.

For in them I meet, unskilled, original, my own hands' shapes,
                    fleet padders, dexterous feet.

For he can run with a dancer's wit, darts of quick-think,
                    finding his feet in a blustery upwind

as he leaps, misses, skids to a stop, all a-quiver to bolt
                    after any lost will o' the wisp.

For asleep, his sonar ears might prick and overhear a star,
                    appraise inflections, apprehend a tear.

For awake, he's all-sense – living's throwaway, unconsidered art,
                    skilled crafter of grace and laughter.

SIGHTING

One step wrong, and she froze to a still,
lost in a grisaille of winter trees,
the slip of a shadow, shy creaturely other –
I stopped to see that darkness clearer.

She might have stepped like fairy from a worn
tapestry of old, or sung by some courtier
hunter-wit for stalking his chamber,

or set by a tree of life which feeds
mosaic water in green and gold
by cooling streams that gleam and whisper.

But I, in the ancient meet we played,
knew I was neither blessed nor graced
but caught on the hoof – and shocked to mirror
myself in her eyes: millennially, a killer.

QUILL

Some creatures come so close to dream,
they cheat the poor insomniac's wake
yet leave a token, spoor or trace –

like *this*, pirnie thing, light as a spill,
this spindly finial, striped beacon,
pliantly sprung as a tapped baton.

What fly-by-night has dropped it here?
as if some phantom trip or synapse
had crossed the brain's nightly relapse

into unthinking – and left for marker
the dart's sharp gift, a cut to the quick,
the wondering thrill of a divining-stick –

so that, by it, you might retrieve
whatever the night's un-sensing missed:
leaf, lunula, quick-fresh, wych –

the dream-words and the dream creatures,
things lost in the mind's discard,
beasts ranging a dark world apart.

I found, this morning, a porcupine's quill,
pied and nibbed, intact and feral –
taper for the dim ways, waking's deferral.

FLUTE FOR THE CHILDREN

Who first notched eyeholes into bone?
and cut the stops, to let the breath
infer the hollow of a note?
      Who thought to blow
          a life through death?
or wish a weeping into moan
             for antidote?

Who heaved a speaking into song?
and blew the sense for calm in storm,
yet sent no news and gave no word
      to keep a hungry
          people warm?
Who played time's beat to right no wrong,
          filched bone, found bird?

THE MOWER

At two, my happiest planet was carpet.
Its catching pile made fine crawler lanes
round curling fronds and furious petals –
Victorian sharawaggi, leading nowhere

beyond the outbacks' floorboards, underlay,
beyond the piano's golden pedal
poking its tongue, the sofa's peepshow:
dust and dark behind a pleated valance.

This was the feeling map of my whole world,
a padded garden of softened blows
laid for those staying close to its ground –

till One came in, tall as a monument,
and all I saw above his shoes' black cups
were the grass-cuttings caught in his turn-ups.

LIVELONG DAY

It's gone thirty years since this light steel disc
                              warmed to his skin,
sixty and more since I laid my child's ear
                         closer to hear
what I could not read (for who goes there?
                    to Babylon, hourly):
my playtime shortened by the whisper of a tick,
                    its sprung mechanism,
light-tongued creature, *touch*-ing, *touch*-ing
                         (so whose time is it?)
his wrist's pale skin, my wondering ear,
                    and I praying
for more time to play, as the calculating thing
                    dialled the sunshine's
livelong light and stole my day
                    with three thin hands –
nothing like hands, but insect feelers
                    that rounded up
my first garden's early dream-time,
                    snaffled away.

Then it was only play-time I'd save
                    from the scuff of its count,
its too smooth run of minutes, hours,
                         its winning way.
Now, finding it silent in a drawer,
               I bend my ear
and wind the tiny tractor wheel
                    to hear it still
touch-ing, *touch*-ing, after thirty years,
                    his wasted wrist

raced to its ending, and the child's child-wish,
                              long vanished, dismissed,
to stay in a garden as light diminished.
                              I strap its cold
close on my wrist-bone, the leather-worn eyelets
                              stretched (almost torn)
to the buckle-tongue, till the fit's my own,
                              my anyone's timing,
and listen – to the doomsday drummer in it –
                              just for a tick.

STILT-JACKS
for Subha

I never saw them *live*, till now
in the hot street, in the beat of drums –
those high personages come from the sky –
what brings them down, stalking for me?
on clippy wooden hoofs, bone shanks –
a lady-lookalike with lipstick smile,
her gawky, lallygagging paramour –
so high, yet they have an eye to me.

Where shall we be once clean off the ground?

SWING SONG

Winging it up, up, in the brace of a frame,
winging it, high as no-holds, into clear air,
scuffing the trodden turf where once a scare,
a hairy centipede, pedalled on too many feet
into my sandpit, stopped, then dived underneath –
so up, higher, disdaining the baby play
of *oopla! oops-a-daisy!* all that sandfall
raining down from handfuls into small hills,
I kicked against my invaded private ground –
flight, my aim: its rise, swipe, rebound –

till something earthy, bone-deep, snagged and jibbed –
a low-down thud that juddered the swing's clean sweep,
shunting up from a fault somewhere at base
where one steel leg had lifted, enough to nudge
the swinging pendulum, and reach where I
had taken wing above the daisied grass,
the breached pen that once seemed close and safe,
the steady ground that kept its secrets dark.
That jolt shot through my arc of pride and wonder,
riding pitfalls of sand, and what lay under.

MARINA
soft sift / In an hourglass... – G.M. Hopkins

Marina, all smiles –
          her two hands cup a miniature landslide.
Seaside child
          preoccupied, lifting and sifting
grains that fall,
          the silk grit of a dissolving ground,
the trick of how
          it spills, wasted, for all her grip.

She scoops a handful –
          (warm sand chuted like a dusty harvest)
and laughs, bemused
          at so much fine stuff running away,
the tease and puzzle
          of things slipping, returning to base.
Elsewhere, sea waits.
          Its taste is salty as a flood of tears.

But Marina makes
          a cradle of hands for each new catch,
finding and missing,
          clutching and losing, raining it through
her fingers' hourglass –
          given, but forfeit, won, but despatched –
then turns up two hands
          (two starfish, startled), empty, abashed.

Sea-child, play on –
            though the game's a no-win losing repeat.
Your riddling fingers
            must outwit your will, filter your finding,
relinquish this gift –
            till the new tide comes and the ruffled sand
readjusts its quilting.
            Don't cry. Go with it. You *will*. Like this ~ ~ ~

LANDINGS

Tucked to the chin in the sand's worn grain,
cradled fast in its stony crumble –
waves, her ancient lully, birth-wail,
earth, her bedding, mineral domain –
these take her in, unaccustomed comforters,
and she, a settler in the sandy wastes,
smiles and plays. I dust the last
yellow granules on her flat-out hand –
a hard packing, ticklish embrace.

Yet fearful, too, having watched that child
scoop hillocks of sand over herself
to make a mummy-mound (Anubis, embalmer,
dog of the dead), but leave exposed
one talking head – old joker to the end –
still smiling, smiling, across the tumulus
of her new hot bed. *Look*, she cries,
outwitting her own disappearing trick:
I'm drowned, buried. No kidding. I'm alive.

And I see (see still) a beach of small mounds,
the dumped refuse of a wrecked cargo –
each body barrelled to a rounded vault,
wrapped, absolved, in its hummocky pad;
and children's faces smiling, smiling,
like lively headstones sharing a joke.
It might be a dream's wild animation:
the sand's soft-fall, light as a plaything,
now heavy as a stone slab to lock them in.

Afterthought:

Could Goya hear – in his painting's dark wit
on the white walls of the *Quinta del Sordo* –
that listening-drowning dog, ear cocked
to catch some voice (from a lord gone deaf)
to halt or explain the unending desert,
the ochre void of an engulfing quicksand?
To drown, landing, is a curse to the sky.
She breathes, and sand-falls trickle either side.
Whose home-ground waits to take so many in?

BY THE BITTER AFRICAN SEA

il mare aspro africano – Luigi Pirandello

Limestone. Flatlands. A deserted beach.
Aleppo pines tormenting the skyline.
This is not a poem I can write, or refute.

A big sea heaves, too bitter to swim.
The keel of a boat draws a line in the sand.
My tongue's in trouble at its very root.

For the long night crossings, too many to count.
Sigh of a keel. Dead children. Landings.
My tongue's unskilled to speak, or confute.

Sea, a strong drink. Sand, soft touch.
What was washed up has been covered, removed.
This is not a poem to sound, or mute.

LYRE FOR THE THIEF

Who first stitched sheep-gut through a shell?
and held it taut to hear the play
of differential lengths come clear?
   Who killed to live?
      yet found a way
to pluck at heartstrings, for a while dispel
        the dread, the fear?

Who touched those guts once nerved to feel?
then coaxed a story, lyricked a mode –
Lydian, Dorian – from a turtle's carapace?
   Who graced the air
     to lighten a load?
then struck a broken chord to heal
      the soul's disgrace?

PICKPOCKET, NAPLES

clever, streetwise, full of guile
cattle-driver, thief by night
— *Hymn to Hermes,* trans. Peter McDonald

I

Lost for a subject, and missing a turn
among flaking billboards, unemptied bins,
pickings for a light touch, legerdemain,
there's an angel's wing flexed at my back –
this artist's quick impersonal tap,
his opportune grace to feel and lift
the obscure object, sweep and scarper,
to dance for a living, no one the wiser,

and I – unaware of my loss, or luck,
a skimming finger at my zipped backpack,
my almost biblically lightened load –
notice too late the exchange of gifts:
a stranger's touch, a poem to start,
and the deal's struck: art for art.

2

Or think another: I walk in a dream
past double-parked lots, boarded-up shops,
a drab street market hustling its cheap stuff,
and chase the ghost of a child that has run
out of time forever – memory's vagrant,
aberrant self – and so miss the touch
of a loss left freely at my back,
an absent given, re-imaginable fact –

and learn how verse comes sideways, adverse,
across the mind's proprietorial hold,
stealing, shy and circumspect,
surprised in the act of finding itself,
a snitch, a cross, neither willed nor desired –
sweet fool, now reckon your soul may be required.

3

The child I was still skulks at my back –
my sidekick, decoy, beggar man, thief,
shill for the trade or *scippatore* –
who dreamed black wolves with red-hot tongues
came streaming out of a molten mouth.
Then pot-luck, fat chance, scat at the double –
Vesuvius cocks a snoop, and waits
its moment, coolly, to take what it can.

Now I salute the child that played
at handy-dandy with nothing to show,
who tapped and ran, or chucked a stone,
or crept, pad-pad, behind Mr Wolf –
yet lay in a sweat of terror at night
for the slipstream beasts, tonguing the last light.

4

And then another: is it I who go
pilfering recalls down memory lane,
feeling for yesterday's no tomorrow?
the creaky funicular swaying to a halt,
blood in a phial liquefying to keep
the moody earth-gods asleep, unmoving,
the simmering mountain sweet, the sea
at bay, at bay, repeating its grief?

Ninna nanna, la luna manca,
sotto il ciel'è buio scuro,
forse un grillo, un lupo mannaro
si perde fra le altre anime perdute.
A catch, a chant against the evil eye.
So Nonna sang for a lullaby.

5

Ninna Nanna, la nonna canta –
sweet janitor of dreams and wake
who bars the door and guards the way
with saints' dust, wolfsbane, song and grace,
who sprigs the pillow, salts the threshold,
kisses the bread that's stale and grey,
and lays a place each day at table
for the son who sickened, who would not stay –

whose bones, one day, she was forced to behold
restored from the soil's volcanic hold,
dried and simplified, coatless, returned
from the dark crossings of earth's old tales.
No *ninna nanna* sung to console
could keep those wolves out of my soul.

6

So beggars all – I, you and they,
our freedom beggared by each needs-be.
I walk these streets, clutching my swag
of savings: bank cards, passport – arts
of being here, passing safely through
each rough demesne: these shop-front blooms
of stained bedding, allotted land-hold
for the church-porch squatters, callers on the Lord.

He'll hear them one day, the *pezzentelle,*
the pleaders, beseechers, too poor for a grave
but rich in the arts of prayer and favour,
whisperers, wheelers, cadgers, singers –
while we who live with the moth and rust
will beg a hearing through their beggars' dust.

7

That sly snapper-up comes quick, tippy-toe,
creeping *behind you*. Don't look now.
Watch where you go – go andantino.
(So *what's the time, Mr Wolf?*
Sand-time, clock-time, star-time, time's up.)
Under the night sky's laughing eyes
shadows lengthen on the beaten track,
fear accumulates like miners' slack.

The longer the road, the nearer they come,
the frighteners feeling for you. Once upon a time
a child outstared the night's blindfold,
keyed the sound of nothing to be heard.
Now, the backdrop creep and halt
of feet won't stop: *look*, pillars of salt.

8

Don't turn, don't look. Forever at my back
the past accumulates, gathers in the shadows
where a long road leaves a trail of leavings:
rat-runs, dustbins, pickings, syringes,
bling and visions, chic and trickery –
all the givens that were lost or filched
on the way, while salt-stacks pile in hindsight
and makes retrospectives from the deadly white.

Keep on, don't look. It's the name of the game:
Grandmother's Footsteps, creepy, touché,
till a wolf in the story – *lupus in fabula* –
cuts across the scene with flaming tongue.
It was fear at the heart – the child's first cue
to ask for answers that will prove fear true.

9

Patron of traders, hustlers, thieves,
lord of the loose tongue, quicksilver feet,
god of the roads, conductor of souls,
wild overseer of dreams and sleep,
heckler, hassler, fantasist, guide,
sweet lyre-strummer, rude street-crier –

Mercury-Hermes, muse of the crafty,
minder of those who nightly bed down
by market trestles, in the tented rigging
of a place left waste, wide open to the sky,
while a whisper of litter will drag old news
through the desolation of the day's after-hours –

grant us, quick-flitter, light-fingered musician,
the art's give-and-take: life forfeit, for a vision.

NEAPOLIS: NUPTIALS

I

As clothes on pegs inhabit their ghost-hang.
As one shoe waits, footless – a clue.
As fugue lurks in the keep of a refuge.

As animal means spirit, although a brute.
As milk might stream through galaxies of stars.
As earth harrows old bones in the marl.

So come to the city of the living-lost.
(Christ, what chance? Three days to rise.)
We'll touch, life-size, our absence-in-waiting

and taste that bittersweet pomegranate, Lady.
The pips are deathly – you know how it is.
Life's a terrible gift to give.

II

Once in, there's no rear view, no road
to check your bearings, chart your route,
or take the compass of a place that's reached

for once, for good, for keeps, for leaving,
the riddle written deep in the skin's
scripted parchment, needled markings.

Once in, you're on your march, and walled
at start and finish, behind, ahead.
No call to answer, no hope to find.

Lady, not a pip or squeak, not a word
can hold out comforts from your underworld.
What's fruited, seeds, and seeds come to fruit.

There's a garden of plenty, a field full of flowers.
Yet the story recalls what the brain disavows:
a girl, abducted, left a shoe to be found.

III

And so, you laid a finger on me,
feather-light as lead. You said: 'this way',
and moaned some ditty in the Lydian mode,

an ancient tongue that touched my own.
And, *hell*, the scene was beautiful, the sea
crumbling blue at the city's feet,

and a mountain plumed to cap the bay's
omega-sweep, its double scoop
pointed by islands either side.

Here, she loosed the wolves in my sleep,
dogs of sorrow that gnaw so deep
they leave a mess of bones, like these

dangling stiltskins in the dimmer crypts,
pauper skulls that crowd for news,
calcium deposits recycling to fuse

with all their ancestors, Romans, Greeks,
generations simplified under our feet.
Lady, must we eat those November seeds?

IV

So I, aged seven, in white socks and veil,
I, dead serious, with a train of tulle
lifted high above my new-shined shoes,

I, all alone, made to walk behind,
in time, not tripping, not dropping my load
of lightweight stuff too white to spoil,

past rows of eyes that knew what they knew,
fears, hints, too dark to discern.
Was I a bridesmaid to the underground?

Or else the usher who walked that aisle
as far as it went, and left them there
side by side, lonelier than I could know,

where the veil I'd carried so high unravelled,
spread far and wide to circle the floor –
its dustsheet thrown over what lay behind.

V

I'd learn, later, how short their time,
how much they knew as they faced away
from those who grieved, and clapped, and smiled.

And I, who accompanied them on the way,
bearing the weight, for life, on my hands
of a trail of white leading to the grave,

half-glimpsed that joker at his party tricks:
wise Pulcinella in black mask and shroud
hatched in my arms as I walked behind.

Little chick, chuck, with your nasal gazoo,
your farty whoops and wheezes, now sing
as you did that day through all our hymns,

and smiles, and veils – for the laughable dark
that waits to take its dues, and inspires
aversion in the blood, prehension of the brain.

VI

As siren's a singer along the shoreline's edge.
As scarper's a slipper left for a sign.
As cryptic opens up to nothing inside.

As Persephone phones from far underground.
As mortal means either living or dead.
As fate's the piecework of three old hags.

Lady, that day you filled my arms
with a gift I neither understood nor desired
but carried to the end, like froth, like fire.

So, come to the city of the living-lost,
long-shored against sudden quakes and faults,
sink-holed into its long history below,

and taste the pips that sharpen the tongue.
That day I bore, too heavy in my arms,
the hard nuptials of knowledge to come.

NAPLES ABSTRACT

So close so dark

      we're daily tombed

a cage of crossroads

      acrostics of stone

no elbow room

      in poverty's strips

dirty pickings

      in quadrant alleys

flushing to where

      (young Caravaggio's

chiaroscuro

      Gesualdo's

Tenebrae)

      sea's a brushstroke

ultramarine

      sky's a cadence

after quarter tones.

      Art's a settling

of murder's scores.

      Blue's a high aim.

Dark's our home.

TOCCATA FOR THE *PEZZENTELLE*

Cittá cantabile, O Partenope –
siren-singer whose song's a despair
                turned over and over,
a wail from earth's fault-line, fluencies of waves,
a corpse knocking onshore for ever –
                a founding in pain.

Neapolis, Naples – shunned enchantress
whose shudder of hurt, like a pulse in the place,
                thrums its bass line
where ancient underworlds press too close,
and the dreamy dead clutter underfoot
                in charnels and crypts –

like these: arranged, efficacious death's-heads,
their wise, wide-eyed, look-alike attention
                lovingly addressed,
polished, wreathed, bedded on silk wraps –
anime pezzentell – soft touch for a petition,
                sweet heavenly pets

cherished for a cure or a lottery win,
held to account in this rough market-trade
                of living and dead.
They might grant a prayer for a shinier pate,
a wish, a grace, for a comfier grave,
                a coin in pay.

Cittá cantabile, Napoli bella –
I come with a new emptiness at heart
                for one lost voice,

and discover the call of an ancient lament
in this cracked earth with its rackety cults
                of death and return,

in the lie of a land that still quakes and kills
and takes us in, with its singing ways,
                to the dead-in-waiting –
where Persephone lurks at a crossroads at night,
Vulcan stokes his volcanic fires,
                Avernus gapes.

So here at the cemetery *delle Fontanelle*
(little fountains at play), I'd touch to summon
                some capped spirit
still shut in its bone-lock of fontanelles,
a life stubbornly inhabiting its matter –
                and pause, bereft.

For see, my own dead are nowhere and nothing,
their lives finished, their voices flown –
                except when I catch
in the tune of an oath, the lilt of an outrage,
such singing sadness in this city's own –
                like her audible ghost.

So I reach a hand – toccata, a touching –
tap for the soul long lost, unnamed,
                riffle a finger
across the anonymous casque of a skull.
For this I'd reach, penny-wish or petition,
                for her voice that's gone.

TASTER

(In the Mother Church of Caltabellotta, Sicily, early Christians
were found buried with coins in their mouths.)

Dream again, tongue. Here's a dead taste:
the shock and cold of that deposit,
the mined metal in the mouth's small pocket.

I can taste you, teaser, like a tarnished wish,
a ticket past all labials, fricatives,
gritty as earth and the hurt earth gives.

I could take my chance and pay my way
with this sour touch of tin or silver
minted fresh from an ancient tender –

like that Christmas sixpence won for luck
which tainted a mouthful of sweetness, and made
its cold contact with the pit and the spade.

How much for the crossing? What do I owe?
On this dry tongue some everlasting metal
might hush a ferryman, tip an angel.

Say, what's the fare from here to over?
This tongue can taste, at no one's table,
that token pass, that price made palatable.

So dream again, tongue. In the mouth's last purse
I'd save one word too precious to waste:
is it *love* or *faith*? Or just that dead taste?

I PUPI

(in the puppet museum, Palermo)

We step inside   and breathe
        dust air
                Who these? we think

hitched mid-swagger on slack strings,
   tacky grandees
in fusty velvet, lacklustre silk,
tin-pot helmets, pearly turbans,
shelved and hung in self's one gesture
drilled for repeats – their purpose set,
   their strung feet groundless.

And yet their eyes – startled amnesiacs –
   stare transfixed,
dreaming the cue that will take them through
old stomping battles, miraculous rescues –
Christians and Moors, dragons and paramours –
till the tale's resolved in the routine pianola's
   drum-rolling tune.

They never sleep, and yet never live –
   unless one night,
touched to lifelike in the light of a beam,
some taut string twitches, some instinct triggers
the aim of a foot, the shiver in a hand, and
(now that endlessly repeating tune)
   hate rattles them again.

We step outside   and breathe
          overhear

                    Who these? they think

ST LUCY'S DAY, SICILY
(for Gillian Beer)

For the sharp clear light of winter, Lucy –
patron of writers, glaziers, and the blind;
for insight tested and foresight tried,
for history's bitter workings-out of strife –

like these rusty spikes, the hardware of war
lodged in the limestone's white knuckle-bones,
Cassibile's armistice, its bombed-out homes,
bunkers derelict among the junipers –

and a forlorn shore of myrtles, dwarf palms,
a lighthouse set to some Athenian fleet
long-defeated, or for Sappho, Plato,
Etna's funny Phrygian cap of snow –

and so, for the dark at the heart of light,
like sad news reaching us here in the sun,
Lucy, grant your lucidity's far sight
for the day, short-lived, and the year's midnight.

A HARROWING

He's got me by the wrist, tight as a clamp,
like a naughty child dragged out of hiding.

No one asked if I wanted this quick way out.
I was happy enough among the asphodels,

at home in the old place, by a forgetful river,
feeling the solid ground under my feet

with the other, unsaved dreamers weighing
all the irresolvable troubles of things.

I'd far rather stay, uncalled, ungraced
in the uncertain shadows, out of the glare

of light, the sky's intolerable vertigo –
conclusive heights I never wanted to climb

where all pain, they say, is repaired, all despair
answered, disasters explained, ever after.

I'd rather linger in these same dim haunts,
lost in surmise and none the wiser

for puzzling the unkind ways of the earth,
close to its roots here, underground.

Perhaps I can slip my wrist from his clutch
and return – to the shades, and fields full of flowers.

THE ICE BEARS
(Rome 1 / 1 / 2020)

They prowl, life-size,
            hunters for a cold and empty nowhere.

They watch with iced eyes.
            Each polar outline's miracled in air's

monoxide warm.
            Children gather (earth's inheritors)

to pat their backs,
            stroke their noses. But love's a killer.

It will melt their hearts,
            scrannel their sinews to drips of glass.

Ice-thickness shrinks.
            In the zoo of our stares their translucence thins

to an empty mirror.
            What inner famine consumes their stand,

distracts their carriage? –
            as if a blurred forgetfulness began

and, shrouded, inexact,
            they clink and splinter, dribble and frack.

Remember sea levels?
            We're fools in wonder. Their lives are pools.

MAP-READING

(Campo Verano Cemetery, Rome)

Like a figured carpet crossed with tees or T's –
an abstract artist's legered grid of strokes,
a child's handwriting practice in straight lines,
a gridlock, head to foot, on a green backdrop –
this bite out of my map shows where names stop.

Embossed, it seems – a mismatched patchwork left
to riddle the city's ultra-literate plan,
a tag or scrap, appliqué, blocking the way
you'd go by some named route – or even (now *read*)
a big speech-bubble stuttering: T T T.

The modern city's crept up on its dead.
A by-pass scores crosswise, ring-fences their edge
in deference to the quiet they must keep.
A railway runs ellipses overhead.
This line marks where the living come to end,

and others – flat-out sentinels unseen –
find storage, cold hiatus – stacked, disposed
in granaries of the imagination's lore.
Not far, they seem, elsewhere. Yet call on them,
you'll cast for roads and leave all maps at home.

WAITING OUTSIDE THE *BAMBINO GESÙ* HOSPITAL

> The shock of a cry –
> then a blue balloon, loosed on its whiplash
> > rippling string,
> queer lung, day-moon, effortlessly roomed
> > in the sky's blue yonder –
> this upstart starter, puff and plaything
> > becomes a prayer,
> an airborne bubble sent forever up,
> > accepted nowhere.
>
> Hard to say
> how far from earth's multitudinous shades
> > its blue will bloom,
> rising on buoyant currents, or fall –
> > for the day is warm.
> Hard to say why one lost balloon
> > in mild December
> should call to mind some child that's far
> > away in a manger.
>
> Here, parents wait
> dumbly, with the bright beasts ranged for sale
> > in a makeshift stall:
> velveteen lambs, donkeys, a lion,
> > creatures made
> to soften a cry in the ward's dark night,
> > assuage a terror.
> Who knows the sweet cheat given of a life?
> > Their glass eyes stare.

STEPS FOR A SARABANDE
(for Jamie Walton, from Rome)

Where a cat scats

        into the foundations

under the moon's

        supercilious eye

(perhaps the cool

        emoji of a smile)

thirty Christmases

        ago we stayed

frozen, laughing

        under the draughty

oculum's cold eye

        sipping brandy

for warmth to sing

        Emmanuel

at the birth of another

        god among them all.

Pan-theon –

        where a busking cello

tonight recalls

        footfalls drawn

da capo from the past

        a solemn-sane

procession of shades

        airborne for courteous

steps and curtseys

        dreamed from a length

of hair that draws

        phrase and form

from the wood's hollow
                    a figure-of-eight
to make a footwork
                    from a ghost's gait.

If any remain
                    lit by this thin moon's
slipper sign
                    stepping into night
may they stay a while
                    aired on a throwaway
scale that climbs
                    stairs to nowhere
from a soundboard floor
                    thrilled out of sight
or a double-stopping
                    haunted chord –
stay till we all go
                    forgetful or foolish
danced or dancing
                    alone to the finish.

TESSERAE

my mother and I were alone, leaning from a window which
overlooked the garden… where we were staying at Ostia.
– St Augustine

A sea of stone heaves over tree roots.
Queer fish spill into grass and weed.
Pale square blocks carry waves in quadrants
where a merman sports a swimming tail
though earth has shifted it out of true,
puckered its scales and smudged its line.
Now he's stone-dry, floored forever,
pocked and dulled by centuries of weather.

A flat-fish pans the sun's round disc.
A snagged Medusa treads huge fronds.
Tentacular as handy flares
her knotty feelers twist and tangle –
she keeps a grim petrific stare.
Elsewhere the picture runs aground
in loose chippings, broken bits
of gods and beasts where nothing fits.

Those pines dig in, and turn their heads.
Might ghosts go tip-toe over these stones?
So Neptune drives his posse of dolphins
under and over, where souls used to go
across the waters, beyond what's dreamed –
riding their drowning, homeward bound.
Now sorrel and vetch unstitch the pieces,
puzzle the point of art's devices.

These cracked wine jars have long run dry.
Marble latrines don't flush their drains.
Was it here he watched his mother die
in a last hotel before the homing sea –
(for Carthage bound, but earthed instead
in Ostia's crowded burial ground),
where dolphins ferry lost souls across a floor –
dream-hardy travellers hoping for a shore?

The day is late, the sun going down.
Small tesserae lost in the burying ground
make small stone tears – for his grief or mine.
I stoop to fit a wedge-angled chip
into the picture, but make nothing of it.
In the setting sun the pines grow darker.
Her absence presses in the bat-quickened light…
How many gather, lapsed into hindsight.

LONG   SHORT   STORY
i.m. Lydia

So   long

long odds

                  long shot

                         long straw

     long   vacation

long-haul

                  long suffering

                         long-stay

      long   finish

                long   wave

           not   long

               so long!

A CALL
'From far, from eve and morning…' – A. E. Housman

And now, from near and nowhere
the phone's ghost silence rings,
and air which steals so many
refrains of familiar voices
spares, for the twinkling of an ear –
(some wide, sky-lit pavilion
a fizmer of wind in the reeds) –
her voice that's nowhere near.

Now here's as far from hearing
and there's no place therefore,
while give's as like forgiving
as call invites recall.
I wait, and dream her nowhere
might still bring nowhere near.

ONE, TWO...

The door swings open on a shaft of light...
Somewhere suspended in that emptiness,
in sun-struck dust, her absence hangs
luminous and still – no ghost but just
a soaring slipway tilted to the sun,
like a going nowhere out of this world
saved, lightly, in the air's warm hold –

just as she'd saved a drawer-full of light bulbs
too dead to shine, a box of alarm clocks,
jam jars packed with biro tops,
aluminium trays, her takeaways stacked
with broken crocks where a sellotaped scrawl
addressed us all – her voice distilled
to a parting shot: 'You are stealing!' she called.

At ninety-four it wasn't fear
but war's self-stinting, and the need to check
the stream of things ever leaving, lost.
Now all these hoarded trifles, wild
inventories of sell-by stuff,
archives of trivia, have turned her rooms
to shadow boxes for quaint heirlooms.

Save something every day, her message,
protect each scrap, each broken gadget,
store the fragile casque of a bulb,
each cracked cup or Christmas wrap,
as if these banked and treasured things
could halt the sly penurious trick
of life, which takes its own gifts back.

Then deep in a musty cupboard I find
half-a-lifetime's footwear marched in rows:
elegant heels, sensible brogues,
old-lady boots cleated and furred –
like grounded hulls dry-docked for repair.
They save the contours of a progress run.
So, how many miles to Babylon?

Perhaps she hoped to stay the drift
of all the waste that's cast by the way?
From heel to toe-cap, tongue to sole,
these empty hubs seem ranged to show
the long road travelled to this glory hole –
where I, now a thief of so much loot,
might speed her onwards, carefree, barefoot...

This blank look of a substantial ghost –
               I know it for a handful,
coddled in a box of scraps and tatters –
               the shed skins
of clothes outgrown, family-wise:
               cambric and ticking,
hodden and gingham, dimity, calico
               (Canopic stuff)
soft to the touch, and topped by that wood-warm
               mute mannikin.

I remember it rocking, egg-head, wooden-top,
               wobbled on a roll.
A child, I'd suck its perfect oval,
               its dummy block,
handle its bland soul, solid and composed
               in a locked capsule.
Now all I see are her hands around it,
               saving what she could
of an old worn sock, its toehold fitting
               like a prisoner's hood.

Seeing the thing, so indestructibly
               complete, intact
on a bed of shoddy – all that remains
               of our childhood's wear:
best and second-best, satin or sack,
               seersucker offcuts

or the taffeta pink of a birthday dress –
                    reminds me how
she'd patch what she could of our lives' reckless
                    wear and mismatch.

After her death we found that basket's
                    crazy bouquet,
its piecemeal sweepings, odds and yard-ends
                    muddled together,
and the egg, set like fount and origin –
                    motherhood's ways
of trying to save the lives she gave –
                    this one hard thing,
and a rag-bag of stuff, scraps, memories,
                    savings against the waste.

PRAISE SONG FOR THE WASHING UP

I wipe the smile from the rim of a cup.
Two spoons cuddle close, groin in groin,
a sexy duplex, a blend of scoops
for a funny mirror – and look, it's you!

A whisk incorporates a floss of egg-white,
empty aspergill trembling for air.
Spatula, ladle, colander, jug,
I'd not mince words but name them clear.

Outside, the world makes news and breaks
so many human bones as it goes.
I try not to break my mother's plates
that clink, gold-rimmed, bone-china thin.

At the bottom of the sink are knives and forks,
and a kitchen devil that carved through meat.
I pick through grease, sponge the blade.
Soapsuds wash off stains of blood.

A robin flusters the bird-bath's water.
Do tines of forks make fangs or prongs,
devil's pitchforks, tridents of an old god?
I strig them clean and feel their teeth.

Sanity is this: this boredom, routine –
that we were not killed, had enough to eat.
Praise for the sweet simplicities of things
that turn no metaphor, imposture no ghosts.

ATTENTION SPAN

A quiet in the house quickens till it's loud.
A palaver in the pipes makes a crowd, on edge.
There's small talk in the water tank, a giggle in the fridge,

and behind them, fainter, some arachnid's finger
picky on a string, or a dust-mote landing
hush, on a windowsill, light as thinking.

How absence tunes the volume higher
like two hands cupped to each far call.
I might hear molecules touch and roll

like tiniest marbles at the heart of things,
a sistrum shuffled in the stuff of matter,
sighs whispered from an air gone quieter.

How absence penetrates, and sets the place
humming at its touch, as if sound's fork
struck elegies in atoms, and then brought forth

incommensurable concerts in our keening ears.
Stone is the sound of it. Now my sense
must span your nowhere in a stonier silence.

Who first stretched calf-skin across a ring?
and snared the edge to make a note
shudder, as if a creature bellowed?
      Who flayed the beast?
           then felt by rote
the beat vibrate against a thing
              racked and hollowed?

Who measured time to thrill the heart?
then set a pulse to lighten the feet
and made a dance-form out of a drill?
      Who paradiddled
          to muddle the beat
until some mallemaroking might start,
             instead of a kill?

ON THE MIRLITON AND THE CLABBY-DOO

Not news, not necessary, not even true,
a promiscuous carry-on, a hullabaloo,
between clabber and clabby, dubh and doo.

These lubberly mussels shelved in sea-rows
make a mirliton of the mirligoes,
a toy pipe burling for an *on-your-toes*.

For a poem's no witness, no errand or view
but might be a caper, carriwitchet or quipu,
like the song of a mirliton and a clabby-doo.

THE OLD MASTERS, AGAIN

About suffering they were never wrong…
– W.H. Auden

About weather they seem a little blind, however,
with their cobalt skies and candy clouds.
Why *no rain?* no dashed cross-hatching
to dim the view and muddy folks' shoes,
swell the rivers and collect in pools,
bedraggle the traveller, divert an angel –
is it an absence of wish or tools?

So Mary's sky-blue wrap assumes
an open highway, quick to heaven.
Below, the three kings glisten like a souk,
a cockerel shows the spectrum of its feathers,
a pedlar walks, his cloak unfurled,
where a clear path winds its exquisite traffic,
beast and commoner, to the ends of the world.

But perhaps no palette can catch the bleared
mirror-ovule of a falling drop,
no grey express the capsuled hollows
of a rainstorm spilling in shaded monochrome.
Is that why no cancellations cross
(like second thoughts) a world all colour,
to fleck the haloes, turn gold to dross?

Or is rain too pencilling, accidental,
a downer on art's sheer dazzle and dare?
A passing shower might spoil the apparel
of the lordly powers, flump their hair,
or wreck perspectives to a heaven inferred.
Outside, we'll take our chance of skies
and go, under weather, dun-coloured, blurred.

CITY, FROM BLACKFRIARS BRIDGE

Among parabolas   earth and architecture
curve and tally   tension and stay
in an arc of glass   its pliable fibre's
photovoltaic   stationary rail-run

I'm high and dry   facing the City's
glittering utensils   toybox of shapes
a dreamscape of fairy   fantastically laid
or a crystal splint   at the heart of an Ice Queen

while under a crooning   intercom of gulls
bent on elsewhere's   immense largesse
a plane's cursor   plots its vanishing
beside the stare-y   sourdough of the moon

and I on my fragile   stop-over toe-hold
my Heraclitean   runway to home
am wrong-footed still   by the lamp-shined slick
of the river slugging   its old luggage of drift.

BRICK WALL
i.m. Roy Fisher

They've no news.
They infest the brickwork. – Roy Fisher, 'A Furnace'

Dear Roy, that day
         you came to read, and stayed sitting
by our pond's low wall,
         composed, considering, I seemed to hear
the long haul
         weighting each word, the footslog in it
driven so far
         beyond your first, original reserve –
like hearing the quicks
         of grass harrowed, deep in the earth.
Dear poet of walls –
         man-made, high-baked, from Tigris, Jericho,
Mohenjo-daro,
         from Roman to redbrick (pissed-on, spray-canned,
scrawled by kids
         with immortal longings), walls blocking
long views beyond –
         how that *Dead acoustic. Dead space*
seems an order to listen.
         Ordinary, oblivious, walls are soundings.

Are you there, Roy?
         where first I met you, in the walls of a poem
so close-up to nowhere
         with its shadowy depressions, mortared holes,
reticulated lines
         of squared-up pieces precisely arranged,
and no conclusions

but just to take our improvisatory
tastes by surprise.
        Are you there? among all the manifest departings,
sightings inferred
        where, for hiding, see? the dead might transfer.
Ghosted to earthworks
        or pearled like tiny nodes of rain,
sucked like damp
        into patinas of brick dust, whitish crystals,
they're a passing stare
        un-remarking, or a thought's rebound
from nothing except
        the clay's absorbent afternoon warm.

Now you've gone
        where the poor of Birmingham, the luckless, the bombed,
the anonymous-forgotten
        linger in the shady brick-work of your words.
Those serviceable blocks
        marked by vanishings, arrested absences,
stored with the form-
        lessness of forms, retain the force-lines
of lives long lost.
        Patched with lichen, topped with stonecrop,
old walls might still
        open a near-view blank and prospect
of shifting souls –
        those invisible drifters, apparent as daylight.
Now you've joined them
        in the bricky exactness of a thing that remains
immutable, finished,
        fired for cladding, impassably proof.
Roy, you're for reading now –
        poems sounding what we don't think we know.

WIND FARM

A pushy wind that fools at doors and locks,
sizing up twigs, loose slates, dustbins, a fence,
for skittles in its noisy knockabout,
will tear chromatic scales from trees and walls
and blow the penny-whistles of their stops,
swiping at all creation's obstacle blocks.

Elsewhere, like rows of yogis synchronised,
the metred wind-farms take their turn to turn
in answering arcades, unhurried rounds –
a plexiform of points that dial thin air
and amplify from weather, power from source
their humming chorus, standing calm in storm.

And so they'll save whatever rage must pass,
storing all that rumpus in small grids
while skinny sails, like wands, access the rush.
Timers, pacers, savers – quick to the charge
their hands' conductors take from a Force 10 gale –
they make lightwork, and hum to the wind's rampage.

HIKE

the here and elsewhere, the elsewhere and here… – David Wheatley

Camino real, or just some peddar's way?
This gravel track inclines to meet the wind
sheered to a blast through a narrow mountain pass,
brushing the hills' snow-bones, their wintry dress –

and always another turn, another climb
towards the imaginary end of a destination.
Running against the clock, my catching two-step
wrests my breath, my heart's trip-up, trip-up,

and no one knows how far it is or near –
hills crowding the distance, summits receding,
and never a map or milestone, shadow or star
to track the passage onwards hour by hour –

only the dry-stone walls whose wandering squares
make open keeps for keeping nothing in,
broken holds for no one's safe returning,
frets to catch the north wind's winter-storming.

Somewhere between the start and an unknown finish
we pause, to sit by a rusty, punch-holed gate,
and hear in it how weariness, patience, panic
sing in the wind's two notes: dominant / tonic.

MAGI

All this was a long time ago, I remember,
And I would do it again... – T.S. Eliot

The camels obeyed us, but each hard step
jarred their baggy, sand-folding feet,

baffled their slow, desert-loving sway,
galled their haughty eastern pride.

And truth to tell, it was a mad-fool journey
chasing a star across unfriendly frontiers,

sleeping by day, riding by night,
lost in wonder at the heavens' design

that showed our going by the constellations,
mapped our passage by the zodiac.

Night after night we measured long miles
by meridians, ellipses – those faraway worlds

winking above us, making a joke
of our insect progress, our extravagant hope.

What reckless gamble was it, to leave
at a dreamer's hunch, the prompting of a star?

only to find at the road's full stop
our wisdom confounded, our knowledge nonplussed.

For the place was nothing but a backstreet stall
where the woman had birthed like a beast in the hay –

a miracle, perhaps, that the child was alive
in all that filth, the mother too,

though pale as a ghost, thin and shaky,
the child asleep in the feeding trough.

We picked our way, hitching our skirts
through a redolent mess of droppings and straw

while some shepherds cursed us, minding their sheep
that fretted and kicked, bleating to get away.

Kneeling was no easy business on that floor,
and to what were we kneeling in that mucky doss-house? –

none of us knew. We'd brought gifts for a king,
but these needed food, water, all the usual

necessities of the poor. We could not speak,
and they smiled politely. Anyway, what's to say?

We spoke another tongue, felt overdressed, ill at ease,
exotica in a poor man's squat,

our fate to glitter in that humble place,
to offer our scents against its homely stench.

Then slow, reluctant, the long trek back –
we were spent, uncertain, our world in reverse

as if turned for viewing too close, too real,
its focus telescoped, its prospect shrunk.

For what had we learned, or gained? – the way
now dark for homing, the landmarks unclear.

That star? Well, who needs stars to show
the homeless with their beasts at the end of the road?

Our soothsayers said we'd find news, a sign,
riding westwards. Maybe they were wrong;

maybe we found it. And what's a find?
Perhaps what is there but not seen before:

the shock of the commonplace, the pitilessly true,
off-track, off-beat, down any blind alley

where you meet the appearance of the merely apparent
and grieve for the lost inspiration of a dream.

So step by step we returned as we came.
We'd forfeited home, abandoned the schools,

forgotten what we knew, and knew nothing more
than this: this sadness lit by a star.

Then turn, and turnabout, by the same stony ways,
the ground harder, sky further, more cold,

and the rest? – a passing without any answer,
our lives, roadworthy, to the end of wonder.

THORN APPLE

Observe this thing: it's yours to keep,
a quartered capsule packed with pips,
some hard commons, certain surfeit –
you'd not eat this, except to die of it.

Who could resist this greenish grenade,
this spiked bauble, pricklyburr,
moonflower's fruit, ticket for a quick-flit? –
you must eat this, though to die of it.

SAGE
i.m. Eugenio Polgovsky, film-maker

Consider a garden, walled and riverrun,
hedged to windward, level-lawned,
flowered in sudden cuts of colour –
a tidy wonderland queering the sunshine.

It seems a formal dreamscape on location,
a take on how the mind might slip
from wide shots back to jump-cuts now,
and loop a blue flower to the afternoon's

routine soundtrack of youthful voices –
futures opening beyond these walls
where we two stop, and pick few words,
feeling along the how's and why's –

as if by some rewound reportage,
the chance of something said, not said,
and all the accidents of happenstance,
it might have gone another way.

So words – pot-shots at what's just hidden,
keepsakes, wake-men, bearers, forbears,
memos, memorials, makeshifts, lightweights,
mystery's lighteners, gravity's weights –

and we who remain talk in a garden...
The air seems thin through which you escaped,
breathable, and all to share;
the sun dabbles in shots of paint.

And here's the blue slipper of a flower
turning a shape as clear as day:
salvia, sage, for safe, safe-keeping,
itself the strange salve of a name –

as if we'd ever know for a moment
what makes a life too hard to bear,
too long to stay, and yet might spare
a word for the light-struck glory of it.

The air is patient with nothing to say.
That blue flower signs, like punctuation,
the place where words break off, and roots
riot darkly across old borders:

salvia, sage – for salvage, saving,
for naming a wish larger than we know,
for wise, or salutary – even, finally,
a salutation: so, *Salve, Eugenio.*

WET SUIT

My feet shove in soft sand's overshoes
shorewards   where

no roots of marram tack the dunes
to hold their ground

but land's an edge   given to alternatives:
wash   and overflow

fluent drag   and measurable erasures
cradling   inwards

where the shining water in sun-struck flashbacks
fathoms its own.

That lens of light sees eye to eye
with the vacuous sky

riveting   and salty to taste.
(Why do you cry?)

You might hear stops like deep breaths of sound:
Tibia   Claribel

Dulciana   Vox Humana
Unda Maris

sweet girls calling   from bones and bells
as each swell   subsides.

I stop   and watch her draw up a sea suit.
Its fishy flipside

will take her in   then quickly insinuate
that cold   filigree

of thinnest water next to her skin –
a dying feel

or shivery tease   in its blood-warmed sheath.
She'll fit   I think.

Then remember another who walked   and walked
into winter sea

her hands tight by the sides of her frock
to hug   within

or else take the carpal cold   to heart
faster   as it seeped

along the speedways of the permeable veins –
a *passe-partout*

unhindered   unrestrained. She'd help the big sea
(no help before)

lift her   clean off her feet as if
to dance or play

to fold and warm   in its icy burn
those light   weights:

the tossed   homing (hurt no longer)
cockles of her heart.

LAST BEQUEST

That steely blade must feel its way
                        through nerves unfeeling,
the incisive knife be guided deep
                        to learn by trial
how the intricate layout, say, of my guts
                        is theirs to track,
both core and prolapse – to haruspicate
                        like Etruscan seers
savvy with entrails, fishing for futures
                        (no longer mine) –
to test bacteria in digested matter,
                        but never to find
the spasm of fear or joy that shoots
                        the wires of the spine.

So this thin skin that makes a permeable
                        mac for sheltering
must split to let the scalpel fetch
                        some future curing
out of a gash, some antidote
                        from the wreck of the flesh.
This outer wrap that keeps me whole –
                        touched by others,
lovers, friends, withheld and lent
                        to the world, its weather –
must suffer blackening into leather.
                        But they'll not mind
my loss of face, my graceless absence
                        when they come in.

They might just tweak my ticklish toes
                that calibrated
countless earth-miles under my feet
                and, keyed to the balancing
bones in my ears, held me upright,
                steadied my going.
Even these hands – quintuplicate tools,
                intelligent utensils –
will not be fussy or flinch but take
                each naming cut:
carpals, metacarpals, phalanges – and suffer
                numbly in good part
such sharp discoveries: how joints and tendons
                ligature a hand.

Perhaps they'll carve the pumps of my lungs,
                those spongy bellows
worked 24-7, and note the knotty
                muscle of my heart –
ugly lump of butcher's discard,
                life's pace-maker,
lovers' medulla, and metaphor.
                Perhaps they'll probe
the grey wormery of the quiet brain,
                mazed to keep
its furious dreams, memorial secrets,
                the logged recalls
of a lifetime's moments, banked to be
                redundant currency.

They'll learn to map this pack of innards,
                  shy to the touch –
their cutlery too subtle for comfort,
                  hooked or scythed
yet sharp to prise the secret landscapes
                  tucked inside.
If I could think this gift of life
                  was mine just by
miraculous pot-luck, its helix spun
                  in a genetic roulette,
I should be glad to hand it back,
                  used and worn,
loved and suffered, to help another
                  in the course to be run.

HORN FOR THE BREATHLESS

Who first put lips to the tip of a horn?
and breathed a cornucopia of sound
to bring the ram's spiral bone to life?
                Who blew the shofar
                        so far around
to waken the dead, receive the unborn
                in time, to strife?

Who raised the slughorn for a clarion call?
and sent an ancient note to warn
of war and exile, plague and hunger?
                Who sounded a flourish
                        only to mourn
the pest that kills, the lives that fall
                in time, by number?

CANDLE

It tongues the wind
for those struck dumb
  twists thin gold
to a wavering tip
  wicks a flaming
keeps its grip.

So wistful, winning,
this antic flare
  makes a symbol
fit for cherishing
  the while consumed
by its own perishing.

And seems a word-
lessness that pleads
  a footling prayer
that hits no mark
  a gleam of hope
that shows the dark.

Like any other
koan or rhyme
  its moment shines
and then goes by
  a mere *sfumato*
in the sky.

And yet, who knows?
this candle spent
    still seems a speaking –
like the dead
    in quietness –
like something said.

THE DEADLINGS

You catch them

          dodging

cold ghost ovals

          honesty pods

crowding like kids

          at windows of the living

like trips and feetings

          leaf-whisperings.

Dear dead

          our outed

friends now othered

          to stars or stories

wherever you are

          outsourced or aftered

skedaddlers dawdling

          in cool betweens

quickeners

          fishing

for a word a line

          like memory's dark side

or grasslands phrased

          by a wind in passing

a lake shadow-played

          by a sky-lit branching.

Attend

        and linger

lend an ear

        or venture nearer

where we the other

        side of ever

search any addresses

        to send a letter.

ROSES / REMEMBRANCE DAY

The late sun glories in these dying leaves.
Ebbtide at sundown's a mirror of pools
rosied – the day's long memory transfused.

The sea makes waves, narrow feint, pale blue.
Someone has strung cut-flowers to wither
at the eleventh hour, for a wayside marker.

A lost breeze shrugs across the buds of gorse.
The landscape makes light work of grief
while yarrow – the last wild flower to keep

its November white – seems a truce, a peace.
Those roses are dead. Their day's brief tomb
leaves yarrow waving where the wind blows through.

A LOST SHOE

When Auschwitz-Belsen was liberated there were 43,000 pairs
of shoes heaped in the camp.

Avernus

So small a thing.
        Just one. Forget it.
                Then start counting
step by step
        the long slope down
                that pooled crater's
roundy way.
        Clutching your *one, O*
                all you own
before death's new
        discourteous slowness
                homing down
the green-fringed lake.
        Note the old phrase
                its sliding *o*:
facilis
        descensus
                Averno.

Chiron

That horse-man trained in music, medicine
                      asked for the stars, slow-dying in pain.

Now Sagittarius speeds his arrow
                  nightly over white fields of yarrow.

Achillea millefolium –
                  salve for the battle-hurt, antibacterium.

Just by the heel she dipped him in.
                    Shoeless, was he? in his Stygian skin.

Earth

Here's a plainness
suddenly strange.
There's white dead-nettle
and yarrow's perennial
efflorescence
salting the ground
of a disused layby.

Memory saves
little of us here
where a tinker's wagon
would park its blithe
toytown horseshoe
and a tethered pony
strayed out of view
on the outshifts of town.

I squat for a piss where
fly agaric
on a rotten pine branch
blooms, florid
as a childhood toadstool
and a woodlouse skids
at loggerheads with
imponderably huge
stops and obstacles.

Deep in last year's
mulch and leaf mould
one leathery tongue
stitched with holes
around the rim
pokes out – tough skin
weather-worn and stiff
but human-formed
to fit. What memories
cluster to it?

So *one is one* –
and somewhere gone
a life, a no-one
known, a long road
on from where
this wasteland keeps
its secrets, saves
odd tokens, leavings
stores life-stories
long forgotten
under yarrow.

Cobbler, cobbler,
mend my shoe.
Romanies, maybe?
wandering tribes,
chance passers-by?
Now, just I
and nothing known
of them. (Yet remember
43,000
pairs of shoes –
countdown to none.)

So I walk on
leaving the yarrow's
healing beds
the white dead-nettle's
absent sting
while deep among them
owned unknown –
(*one is one*) –
that silent tongue
speaks volumes, calls
multitudes now dumb.
Whose shoe in the mud?

THE MARCHLANDS

Their tiptoes dabble in our mortal zone – halfway markers,
                     aimless feelers in pedestrian air.

Do they dream of gravity? flying in lightweight windy clothes,
                     massed for a sunset, ferrying messages.

Mostly they hover on the engine of their wings, feet dangling –
                     slack puppets loose from their strings.

Sometimes they sing – notes like humming-tops' thin harmonics,
                     wheels shimmering like Jupiter's rings,

or loll in marble across high altars, bare legs trailing
                     out of the frame, over the edge,

teasing the solid ground beneath, feeling for us
                     earthbound marchers, heavy in our limbs.

Or else they haul clean startled bodies out of their graves,
                     disturbing earth's cover of stone and mud.

But here's no place for seraphic ways. Not theirs the road
                     that must go nowhere on, and on,

history's marchlands — and a drumming savage in the human brain,
                     numerate killer addicted to sums:

one thousand, two – (think, Celan's 'Death Fugue', Radnóti's 'Forced March') –
                     the Jew-ditch dug, the pot-shot triggered,

the long march driven to the pit's last step – a staggered finish –
and earth a trap, a crowd, a cover-up.

No angel foots it in those dirty troughs. Too high and dry
they wing free in dream and fable,

unimaginable. Out of the deep, cry counts of millions –
walkers death-marched to the ditches we dig

out of race, nation. They trip off the tongue. Such passports claim us.
Will an angel land on the graves we make?

ISOLATING

I forgot my self – and soon learned not to miss her.
She was wounded, angry at first, bawling for attention.
Gradually she tired, pausing, and the pause entered in
like another conversation. The pause said a kind of nothing
profoundly, like the drop of a well that is dry and endless,
an auditorium of fall, the hollow vortex of a horn.

It seemed the sound-form of a world plunged in quiet,
so I heard the push of a cowslip, squirrel-gifts in the lawn,
the crying loneliness of someone stopped at a window,
and pain like a hum, pitched deep in the human brain.
Yet something on the thin tympanum of the ear still tapped
to come in – a counting game, first one, then two,

for all the world's mute calls, its momentous news:
it was only a pause – steady on – the small-talk of a poem.

THE ART OF SPACE

Consider the art of space.

A tree fielding blue air.

Debate of oxygen, leaf –

our crucible atmosphere.

Fine words in a race of breath.

Then pinned on paper to make

debate of art and worth –

each branch and root at stake.

Consider a pause for sleep.

The dream's roomier instinct.

Debate of pulse and brain –

then waking's carbon footprint.

HYMN FOR A TREE

Sentry to the heavens, archangel tree.
Breather, ventilator – CO_2
converter. Stay. Give us this day
our breath. In times of pestilence, renew.

Green aerial, mesh for cosmopolitan air.
Bearer, silencer – exhaust emissions'
neutraliser. Lend us your leaf-lungs.
Creation's miscreants, we learn hard lessons.

You're subterranean, a secret sharer,
communicator by touch and reach.
So breathe, for us who choke, who want
to know, and grasp too little, too much.

I go all about. You take your stand
and deepen down to darkness underground.
I'm double-helixed, spindle-shanked.
My thoughts tend word-wise, spiral-bound.

But you teach stillness to the roots of things.
Fanner, inspirer – the breath you give
(a chorale of singers repairing the air)
is all the breath by which we live.

Chlorophyll-maker, angel rainer.
Guard of the near-view, the minuscule, the slow
co-operative way of life's survival.
Stand by. We need you – the breathless. Grow.

IN TIMES OF PESTILENCE, EASTER 2020

supposing him to be the gardener – John 20:15

like rising early to a garden – stealing
a march on daylight, surprised in its hiding,

like finding the fly-away, pink and white
cutwork of a cyclamen winged for no flight,

the tenter of a fine web, or silver chains
of glittering jewellery cast by a slug,

like figuring a world first dreamed as leaf-work
turned to the sun, and a tree lording it

oh, so lightly – while, fresh as surmise,
a figure absents itself, and the place,

greened and eastering, gives no sign,
saves no memory of a touching scene

buried in story, hard to recognise.
And yet the recalcitrant mind still dreams…

of rising early to a garden, snatching
time before the time that makes

its daily count of living and dying,
a mounting tally (some grim auctioneer's),

while through the sunlit shadows the gardener,
lost in supposition, also disappears.

BREATH

Breath   a backslap shock   a wallop-
ing gasp for starters   bellows for a cry
the lightest thing   to weight us   yet
a ponderable gift   live-in tenant.

It's donkeywork   a non-stop treadmill
ins   and outs   hoovering the blood
sifter   pumper   porter   singer
love's transporter   spirit's figure

thinking's   wish   on the fipple of the tongue
tell-tale whispers   from psyche   anima
cagey inspirer   airy designer
of phrases   syllables   a lifetime's timer.

Till quiet   as unheard consonants   a sigh
spires to the winds   for a last   sound crossing.

JANÁČEK'S NOTES
(as he notated his daughter's dying breaths)

I time you, dearest, to the last minute now,
hold your departing to a page of notes,
scribble each phrase your breathing makes
in breves, minims, in the pause between
each catch, acciaccatura, of your breath –
its stress and start, then a rest – rest.
I hear its sparing quiet on your chest.

I time you, living, to save your breath,
Olga, Jenufa, in the world's free air
that's large enough to sustain the tune
we make, breathing, still lightly keeping
time for a time till, two against three,
these sudden faint syncopations misalign,
and you're out – on a beat much wider than mine.

I compose you, darling, in this plot of time,
the sigh of oxygen sieved through your lungs,
the wheeze and panic of it flying free
beyond my shaky amanuensis hands
into the open, unaccompanied there –
your solo-silence towering, avant-garde,
while I re-arrange these notes in a graveyard.

A COUNTING SONG
(in times of Corona Virus)

It was dusk, late April, but midsummer warm.
Through the reeds it sounded: *who? oh.*
Who knows? translations of a ghost in note-form.
That day no-one spoke for unspeakable sorrow.

Perhaps all I heard was a wing on a thermal
or a five-barred gate in the breeze expel
a conch-shell's harmonic, low glottal.
A sound-thought carries further than a yell.

The comma of a moon made a curb or crook.
Friend, are you there? Here's a pause for breath.
Nothing is written in the sky's darkening book.
Self's *who?* sorrow's *oh.* And the silence underneath.

From a reedy outcrop fringing the void
                              one note. Then stop.

It seems the faintest apparition of a noise
                              a presence caught

on the brink of the imagined. Perhaps a voice
                              tuning to call

or a dreamy upbeat, the point of a silence.
                              (Friend, is it yours?)

The only music in a silent time
                              unaccompanied moan.

One – was it one? Like the stroke of a bell
                              mechanical, deadpan.

Then nothing. A tease. (The musicians are silent
                              the concerts forbidden

the world listens to multitudinous breaths
                              gasping for air.)

Then two, two notes. Like a rumour starting
                              to fret along a nerve.

Sad slow tymps for a marche funèbre
                              pitched and counting.

Or else a bassoon warming its woodwork
                              punctual, hooey,

inexpressive as a practice-drill.
                              Then I remember

what I knew, forgotten, a word for the thing:
                              bittern that rare bird.

observed from any that walketh the fens
                              Thomas Browne averred.

(*Pseudodoxia Epidemica.*
                              It was plague time then.)

The physician-poet noted this same
                              refrain from nowhere

earth's auscultation, seismic, probing.

> A low pulse in things.

No tune, but just a counting rhyme

> a rhythm in time

like *two, two, the lilywhite boys.*

> (Was it someone you knew?)

(Friend, are you there where they count in thousands

> names and lives

where breath comes hard, missing its cue?)

> These flats lie quiet.

Earth's a footnote under loaded skies.

> A star sends a sign.

And I listen again for that woodwind entry:

> two, and counting.

(No music played where breath's too short

> to sound a note.)

But *a bittor maketh that mugient noise*

> the physician observed

the poet improvised: *mugient* – a moo.

> No sound now crosses

the comb of rushes that strokes the horizon.

> There's nothing to see

in those grassy screens twitched by the hold
                              of a shifty bird

that clambers, freezes, in the reedy stalks
                              invisibly cryptic

streaked and pointing. Then another note shocks
                              the deepening dusk

half bump, half boom, a queer ventriloquism.
                              That calling gong

repeats its tally: three, four.
                              Four for a ghost-breath.

(Friend, can you hear the unsinging bird?
                              its bottled-up summons?)

I breathe deep in as if I could save
                              some air, music

to replenish your store, feed the supply
                              you need to live.

the inspiration or hailing in of air,
                              affordeth a sound –

the physician surmised. No flutey flutter-tongued
                              circular breathing

but a slow peristaltic lunge or gulp
                              a burp or hiccough.

I hear that pondering note repeat

>
> five times. Then pause.

Five for the symbols at your door.

>
> Five, a quincunx.

A full-fathom-five of notes implore

>
> like something lost

the tiny godhead of a pathogen run

>
> amok in the bloodstream.

Five for the symbols: pentagram or Passion?

>
> Or just five knocks

at the door's blank face that shuts you from us.

>
> (You breathe in numbers, friend

clocked and checked.) *Acute respiratory*

>
> *distress syndrome.*

But *distress* too light for the high-tec monitored
>
> life or death

you suffer, beside the digital tick-

>
> tock that silently

works your lungs: trachea, bronchus,

>
> pleura, alveolus.

The physician laboured (it was plague time then)

>
> and wrote his case notes

composed his prose to the rise and fall
of a breathing rhythm:

The sicknesse which God so long withheld from us
is now in Norwich —

letter to his son, 22 September
1665.

The counting rhyme that counts us in,
and out, must time

the lungs that hurt, the heart that skips
the tunes we hum

the words we pick. I send this greeting
in time, like them,

across the fens that feather the skies
with *rushes, O.*

Friend, can you hear these sound crossings
these calling pips?

The bird that has no song to sing
hones one note.

Then stops… to let the quiet carry
extempore.

Perhaps your magician ear might shape
old hearsays of us

in the locked smiddy of your listening where
                                    that bony blacksmith

hammers the silence to a dream memory
                                    a hallucinating rhythm.

As when the music ends you hear
                                    the architecture

of a wished intention, a finish extended
                                    memorised as gift.

Friend, can you hear? the beat that seconds us
                                    by the minute

the count that repeats repeats repeats
                                    beneath our melodies

litanies, tom-toms, the heart's dance feet.
                                    And then this bird…

that seems a wishing in the night's dark cover
                                    and ghosts a prayer.

Flesh – sweet intimate, gansey, gyp.

I is the brief composite of this scatter.
Now flush in the sunlight, emerging live,
the wondering engine walks its rope.
(Fifty neurotransmitters to report.)
I is the stake that holds it taut.

This weight-lifting arm's a crane and winch.
Each leg propels on tendon pulleys.
Shock-absorber feet must pace, and spread
(twenty-six bones, thirty-three joints)
grappling toes to the underlying cold.

This knobby back-stick's packed with fascicles,
notched like a wand, a magic nerve-stick.
The brain's top-heavy fastness contains
(a hundred billion neurons crossing)
jump-leads of dream, logic, wit.

And I, a breather pieced in time,
crucial, upright, a thing apart,
now walk alive, *alive*, and feel
(thirty-one pairs of spinal nerves)
that old niggle, small stone in a pocket:

soul – sweet amulet, wishbone, riddle.

A LIGHTHOUSE

i.m. Anne Stevenson

'Ariel flutters', you wrote, misquoting
the doctor's report, and I laughed to think
of the tricksy spirit flexing in your heart,
its wit and spite, though pining to leave
the timed sentence of a life's work.

Now I watch this metronome of light
swiping across the absent-minded stars –
their nearly nowhere, like homing cats' eyes –
and dream some Ariel still flutters free
of the heart's two-feet, the mind's last rhyme.

RETURN TO THE SEA

No floats or buoys.
Now go   released from marching orders
free of your bones   noseying below

the opalescent shine
where sea says nothing   over and over
a stray arithmetic   lapsed from time

where sirens travel
the long-haul weathers of all the world
intercontinental   outre-tombe.

So I'll unravel
like weed in the shallows   rags in the wind
stretch   like meniscus on a longshore drift

and leave behind
the steadying rhythms   the count of the clock:
age   date   origins   name.

I'll take that first step
clean out of step   my kilter knocked
by a big sea-shoulder throwing its weight

then sink to swim
far out   with lung-sacs full of the sky
eyes   fixed on some far-out island.

For sea's the slipper
of a footing missed   a quicksand trip.
It fits all comers that cede their ground

in the lift and toss
the long sound crossings   of the lost   the drowned
a singing glossa   multiple tongues.

LAST THING

Each night, last thing, I touch your shoulder blade –
a hold on what's so fragile, so unsafe –
and wonder how, you gone before I leave,
I'll wing it, then, into the world of dream.

TOWARDS TRANSLATION

DANTE, 'PURGATORIO'
Canto X, 1 – 48 (Literal translation)

Then as we made our way through that door
which the soul's unwise, earthly desires
disable quite, so a wrong path seems right,

I heard it clang resonantly shut.
If then I'd turned to look back in regret
what could have excused my disobedient heart?

We climbed up higher through a stony fissure
that rocked first one way, then another,
like a wave concussing in ebb and flow.

'Here we must employ a modicum of art,'
my leader began, 'in edging close,
this way or that, by the side which rolls.'

And so we went with such cautious steps
that not before the waning moon
had snuggled down in her darkening bed

did we clear the gap in that needle's-eye pass.
But once we were out and free of danger,
up where the mountain levelled to a plain,

I, quite exhausted, and both of us still
uncertain where to step, we rested on the flat –
a road lonelier than any desert track.

And from that edge which gives onto nothingness,
to the foot of the rise that rises higher still,
the measure was just three lengths of a man;

though as far as my eye could see to scan
either by the left side or the right,
that circling plateau stretched an equal span.

We'd not yet started to trudge uphill
when I perceived that, all around,
the bank rose sheer, abrupt and pathless,

and the Parian marble was adorned with reliefs
that might have outdone, not only Polyclitus'
chiselled art, but nature's own.

The angel, who came to earth with news
decreeing the age-long, wept-for peace,
unlocking the sky's old barrier to heaven,

appeared so lifelike beside us there,
and sculpted with such a graceful sweep,
it seemed an image about to speak.

One might have sworn he cried: 'Ave!'
For there, imaginatively carved, was the one
who turned the key, unlocking God's love.

Her very stance seemed to tell the tale:
'Behold the handmaid of the Lord' – just so
an imprint sets its seal in wax.

DANTE: ON REFLECTION

(verse commentary on Purgatorio, Canto X, 1 – 45)

So this is the way to go, however
you summarise the sin, calibrate the soul:
to follow a road to the ends of the world.

That door clanged shut – was I out or in?
(Over my shoulder Eurydice lapsed.
Lot's wife was salted to an upright stack.)

But he and I pressed on through a chink –
stonewalled, yet finding some permissive path
that pitched and rolled under our feet.

My dear poet warned me: 'Now use your art.
Just dance, balance – dare to dream
how a passage might carry you through and out.'

It was madness, I knew – sheer lunacy to think
we could find our way in the waning moonlight,
squeeze our shapes through the eye of a needle

to clear this world and discover another.
But we did, somehow, emerging elsewhere
on a plain, a blank, a flatness so sheer

we stepped out blindly, trying to find our feet,
dizzied by a ground that stretched to nowhere –
lonely as hell, barren as a waste.

And though it seemed endless, measureless to man,
yet a mountain rose, and near where we sat
an edge gave suddenly onto nothingness.

I searched the fathomless scene all round,
trying to map that country of the mind,
its wild carousel of heights and depths;

and then I saw, suddenly quite close,
a cliff of white rising beside me.
Impassable it seemed, a marble sheet,

but beautifully, finely carved in relief,
finer than porcelain, sharper than light,
than icicles shaped by nature overnight.

And I traced an angel with the grace of a man
announcing *All Hail*, wings riffled with flight.
The words in my ears from the hollow of his mouth

matched my deepest heart's desire –
as if the scappled marble sliced
sounds out of air – was it memory's knife? –

and a palombino whiteness met
like breathlessness my outstretched hand.
I could dream-caress each dumb-found sense.

In death's harsh land of pain and penitence,
where sweating, wounded souls staggered up
their helix track – sorry flesh-bound shades

bound for the summit to be freed from themselves –
I paused to follow the stone's allure,
its speaking lines figuring a cry

ancient as story, rehearsed every day
in wishing litanies, faithful prayers.
And then I remembered my own art's hoard

of echoes gathered from ages before:
the river from which no soul returns;
three times that shade fled, fugitive as dream.

My sweet poet nudged me. It was time to go,
but I ducked, delayed, slunk round to stay
gazing at that angel's momentous invitation:

to sing death's *ninna-nanna* to a child;
while, pierced with foresight any mother denies,
she knelt to answer with heart-broken eyes.

So something truer than right or wrong,
than measured dues and heavenly rewards,
gave me pause – and held me dreaming, where

that marble effigy gentled the cliff face.
How know art's knowhow, its slow skill to feel?
Where else but elsewhere is the dream's own place?

I searched sin's calculus, to discover art's grace.

I
La Via / The Way

   Lonely house, at the heart of my native land,
here on an airy plateau of blue clay
to which the bitter African sea
sends a flurry of foam, whisperingly--

   you, I see, forever from afar
if I think of the spot from which my life,
so tiny, opened on the world's futility.
From here – I can say – from here I made my way.

   From this little path that runs between olives,
scented with wild mint and perfumed sage,
I set out for the world, ignorant and artless.

   And far and wide, O little shy flowers
hidden among hedgerows--so far I've trudged
only to return, disillusioned and weary.

II
Rifugio / Refuge

The mulberry? Long gone. There's only the mass
of tiger-striped rock where I sat, shade-hidden.
Wandering, indefinite thoughts once troubled
my infant soul, fleeting as air.
Secret pleasures, fears of the unknown!
Were leaves of a branch really its wings?
Did longing to fly make them glisten so?

My own tentative desires, half-fledged,
palpitated thus, not yet winged.

Perhaps this tangle of wild mint is the same?
It perfumes my hand with a sharp fragrance,
and I savour again the taste of those days.
I'd run, happily, to hide in this place.
Then hidden, call out my name to its echo,
pierced by a mysterious pang to hear
the mountain call me back again,
lugubriously. I'd think out loud,
naively believing that the trees, the blades
of grass, the dark green ferns and rosy
heathers – all could hear me. But perhaps,
in fact, they couldn't speak my language?
That mulberry caressed my head with its leaves –
friend and protector: 'Little boy,' it advised,
'use reason, yes…but much better to sing…'
And the flowers lifted up their heads again,
marvelling at my song.
Often I'd linger in this spot long hours,
helping the ants climb higher up that rock;
but they were mistrustful, fearful of help.
In truth, they wanted to fend for themselves…
How different from men…
              Where am I? I was reading.
Here on the rock the book lies open.
The wind gets up. Furiously,
it leafs through the pages.
So all is read. All vanity!

ATTESA / WAITING

I am like the tree that awaits
its season, and meanwhile looks dead.
Some lively little tit comes by to ask:
'Still waiting, tree? Time's up – make a move!'
But the tree takes no notice of the chattering tits.
Mute and absorbed, it dreams on and on.

It dreams fresh shoots – that its branches will,
with luck, accommodate the rarer flight
of a precious guest: a nightingale.
No longer will the calls of other birds be heard.
There's a moon in the sky; and a magical lacework
of shadow-branches imprinted on the earth.

It dreams and dreams... But perhaps, already,
its season has passed, and the tree waits in vain,
or perhaps it will never leaf again...
O tree, if this has been our very last
icy spell of winter weather,
what lovely dreams the axe must fell!

INGRESSO / ENTRANCE

At the entrance to life,
fearful, I peered round
a half-closed door.
I rapped with two fingers,
then courteously enquired:
'May I? Excuse me…
    May I enter or not?…' Silence.

So very very gently I push open the door.
Pitch black. I smile,
but feel a freezing start within me.
'Can life be dead already?' I think.
I grope; stumble; then a horrible shriek
fills me with terror:
    'Can't you see? Watch out! You pesky wretch!'

Who now would waste even a match
on that point-blank wall of total dark?
At last, a glimmer. Slowly I make out
a dirty old crone, an ugly witch
peering at me: 'So, who the hell are you?'
'Well,' I answer, 'I am sorry
    to be a nuisance…

I am one who has only just arrived.
Is it late? Perhaps on the journey here
I lost my way…
However, if possible, and with permission,
but only in passing and quick as a flash,
I'd like to visit life, if I may.
    I'll be gone very soon…'

'What, you too? you too have a yen
to enter life? You silly fool!
What do you expect? tell me now…
Have you, then, nothing better to do?'
I stand open-mouthed, staring like a gawk,
and reply: 'Well… I don't know…
   I don't know anything…really…'

'Huh, so I see!' the old witch continued.
'Then take your chance, draw your lot,
and good luck to you!
Before they enter, all who arrive
help themselves to some heavy burden,
some sad misfortune from this enormous box.
   You know the old story

of Prometheus and Pandora?
Go on then, take it. The box is here.
I am Pandora, ancient
and accursed! living still
and reduced to this
door-keeping drudgery.
   Enough! Have you got it? Now get a move on!'

And so I plunged my trembling hand
into that huge, obscure cavity,
and fished out my fate.
Then I entered… Alas, I've seen
so many evils now, I no longer care
to know which one's my own special pass
for entering a life that can only come to pass.

Hey you, you living as I am, even you –
you for an age, I, thankfully, just for a moment.
But I see you and think of you; you see nothing
and, bless you! don't think, but creep to my feet,
approaching close with a submissive roar,
unravelling a bolt of foam, gentle beast.

Like a seller of lace… Bravo! Bravo!
You lay out a sample, then quickly withdraw it,
and here's another, and another… You fool,
is this how you use your power, lazy dolt?
Have a go, try other tricks… surely you know some?
Why, swallow up the whole wide earth, for one!

LA FUNE / THE ROPE

Master rope-makers, a curious business,
yours; going always backward so
on that rope issuing from a calloused hand,
and never deviating, even by an inch.

And yet, come to think of it, everyone must
bite the dust, cry for the moon,
our way's no different perhaps from your own.
We draw out life as you draw a rope.

The wheel, from which an uncertain thread twists
to steady us now, is always in the past;
and we go ever on, backs to the future,
nothing ours to be seen in advance.

Master rope-makers, far too rapidly
turns my wheel, too twisty my rope,
too rough on my hand that tugs at it here.
Why, I'll make a slip-knot, and pop my head in it.

IMPROVVISI / IMPROMPTUS

I

Who says that time must fly?
Why, time flying is nothing at all.
I see you now as when you were a girl,
     Maria Lembo,
   in your new silk dress,
   blue-and-white striped,
under the winged, garlanded brim
   of your wide straw hat.
You see, time flies no longer.

They've told me you're dead;
but you were old and it's no matter.
I too am old, Maria, I too,
but just now I'm still young with you
   at the Casino Valadier
on that broad terrace overlooking all Rome.
You want to know where Tordinona is,
Tordinona that no longer exists.
There it is, I say; now never fear
that your aunt might see you
alone with me.

11

I live in the dream of a shadow in water –
shadow of green branches, and houses down there
all topsy-turvy, and new young clouds… and
everything trembles: the white corner of a wall
on the dazzling blue of the sky, a rope
cut across it, a streetlamp, the black
        trunk of a tree,
        sliced by a sheet
of yellow paper that floats lightly by…
Shadow in the water – liquid city…
    a tremor that shines, immensity of clear sky,
        and the green   green   green
of leaves – everything seeming to come and go,
        alive without knowing.
Water does not know, trees do not know,
neither sky nor houses… Only
a poor fellow knows it all, going alone
    along the melancholy bank
        of the canal.

VISITA / VISIT

Hatching fancies is also something...

      Companions mine, crickets under the stars,
still singing in monotone without a pause;
     why, I'll skip to see what that light is, over there –
who knows? by chance it might be day.
     In four hops I'm off, and back again.

    There was... no knowing what I saw: a rumpus!
     mad shouts, a racket, chairs on the floor.
It's there! – they shouted – *Here! Stop, I'll catch it!* –
     The lamp shattered, and in the dark it was war... –
Quiet! A light! The bride has fainted! –

Hatching fancies is also some thing...

A CRICKET FOR PIRANDELLO
for Roger Pearson

Nascere grilli è pure qualche cosa… – Pirandello

Our trade's translation, whether poems or prose –
and here in Rome
struggling to render Pirandello's 'crickets'
I must lose the creature or else the dream,
meaning's gravity or else the grace.
Nascere grilli, he writes, to signify
fancies, daydreams, born on the hop…
but no insect makes a leap that's fit
for Englishing that device of wit.

So here's a leap-poem, Roger. It goes
channel-hopping
from me to you, scrambling the frontiers –
since we who traffic from tongue to tongue,
mother to other, native to strange,
must make thought's impulse dance to the tune
that words call, by whims of their own:
idiom or pun, some self-stranging homonym,
the distant phones that ring in a phoneme.

Now skip: think ragwort, that hardy immigrant,
taking root
in Oxford's first botanical garden,
later, on Isambard's cinder-tracks
riding westwards, seeding the dry ways –
but remembering still in the rails' sapped clinker
how once it rode the charcoal flows
of Etna's pyroclastic scree –
one hop ahead, gold-gracing earth's gravity.

So *Nascere grilli...* On a Sicilian plain
small jumping jacks,
blue and orange in the hot afternoons,
would gleam beside his rockfast tomb –
flashes of insight, lost as seen.
We'll dream, so words go jumping free
from page to eye, from mouth to ear,
and hatch wild fancies in translation –
cricket-strangers on the ground's foundation.

NOTES

Stormy Petrel – The name may be etymologically related to St Peter who (briefly) walked on the water, or be a corruption of 'pitteral' from the pitter-patter of the bird's feet on the sea surface.

Humming-Bird Hawk-Moth – The quotations and stage direction, '*Enter... Moth*', are from *A Midsummer Night's Dream*.

Saving his Gloves – 'nunkey tumps' is a Yorkshire term for large molehills.

Landings – Goya's 'dog in a quicksand' was painted on the walls of the '*Quinta del Sordo*', the house of the deaf man, where the painter was living.

Pickpocket, Naples 3 – '*scippatore*', Neapolitan for bag-snatcher or thief.

Pickpocket, Naples 4 – The Italian is mine, and translates literally as:
    Ninna nanna, the moon's not here,
    under the heavens it's black as night,
    perhaps a cricket, or else a werewolf,
    is lost among other lost souls on the way.

Pickpocket, Naples 5 – the Italian translates as 'grandmother sings'.

Pickpocket, Naples 6 – '*pezzentelle*', see 'Toccata for the Pezzentelle'.

Pickpocket, Naples 8 – '*lupus in fabula*', Latin proverb, 'the wolf in the story', which translates as 'speak of the devil'.

Neapolis: Nuptials – 'the Lady' is Persephone, whose eating of pomegranate seeds after her abduction by Hades resulted in her being returned to the upper world only for a part of each year. The legend that she left a shoe behind to signal her return has little foundation, unless the unexplained shoe in the fresco at the *Villa dei Misteri* in Pompeii has something to do with it. A Neapolitan legend, however, associates her with the statue of the Madonna di Piedigrotta who, it is said. rushed back into church after rescuing some stricken sailors, and lost a shoe on the beach. (Cinderella, by the way, is also originally a Neapolitan tale.)

'Pulcinella' – the comic wise-fool from Neapolitan *Commedia del Arte*, whose black mask and white shrouding outfit associate him with death, as well as laughter.

Toccata for the *Pezzentelle* – The '*anime pezzentelle*' are the unknown pauper dead, whose skulls are gathered in three large caves in Naples. They were traditionally tended by the living in return for favours granted – a practice surviving despite a ban by the Church. Such tending might involve giving them a special niche, polishing their skulls, or sometimes leaving a coin to help them on their way to the next world.

Partenope – the siren-founder of the city, whose body was washed up on the shores of Naples after she was rejected by Odysseus.

Vulcan – the god of forges and fires, often located in volcanoes like Vesuvius.

Avernus – according to Virgil, this lake outside Naples was the entrance to the underworld.

St Lucy's Day, Sicily – Cassibile is the small town where, in 1943, the armistice was signed which surrendered Italy to the Allies, with disastrous consequences for Italian troops in the north and elsewhere.

On the Mirliton and the Clabby-Doo – mirliton is a toy reed pipe; clabby-doo (from the Gaelic *dubh* meaning dark) is a large black mussel. The mirligoes means dizziness.

Thorn Apple –the very poisonous fruit of the dattura plant.

The Marchlands – On a final death march, the Hungarian poet, Miklós Radnóti, was shot and buried in the mass grave he helped to dig. His notebook of last poems was discovered in his pocket when, some twenty months later, the body was exhumed.

A Lost Shoe – *'facilis descensus Averno'* (Virgil) translates as: the way down through Avernus is easy. For Avernus, see *'Toccata for the Pezzentelle'*.

Chiron – the god of medicine and music, who taught Achilles the arts of healing, in particular the use of yarrow as an antiseptic in battle. But being wounded by an arrow himself, was in such pain that he forfeited his divinity and was turned into the constellation, Sagittarius.

Achilles – was dipped in the river Styx by his mother to render him impervious to wounding, except the heel by which he was held.

yarrow – appropriately the Latin name for this plant is *Achillea Millefolium*.

A Counting Song – *Corona Virus* – the deadly pandemic of 2020.

boom of the bittern – the unearthly mating call of this fenland bird.

observed from any that walketh the fens – this, and other quotes, are from the works of Thomas Browne, physician, naturalist and writer, who lived and worked through the Great Plague of 1655–56, and who kept a pet bittern. He speculated about the mechanism of its cry, surmising that it was produced by an inhalation, not exhalation, of breath. In fact the bittern's boom, up to five tremulous notes at a time, issues not from the wind-pipe but the oesophagus.

two, two, the lilywhite boys and *Five for the symbols at your door* – from the counting song that runs through this volume, 'Green Grow the Rushes, O'.

Acute respiratory distress syndrome – the often fatal condition caused by a severe reaction to the form of Corona Virus known as Covid-19.

Dante: On Reflection – 'he and I' refers to Dante's companion, Virgil.

the river from which no soul returns;
three times that shade fled, fugitive as dream. – Quotations from Virgil's *Aeneid*.

A Cricket for Pirandello – *Nascere grilli è pure qualche cosa,* from Pirandello's poem, 'Visita / Visit'. I render it as 'hatching fancies is also something'. '*grilli*' is untranslatable because it means crickets, but also whims, fantasies, fancies.

ACKNOWLEDGEMENTS

Warmest thanks to all who have read and commented on
these poems, either the whole volume or individual poems.
Special thanks to John Kerrigan, Anne Stevenson, Sasha
Dugdale and Robin Holloway, but also to Harriet Marland,
Andrew McNeillie, Subha Mukherji and David Wheatley.
Editors of various journals have been invaluable responders
and tweakers of lines. Finally, Michael Schmidt has, as
ever, been a wonderfully supportive, scrupulous editor. John
McAuliffe read the manuscript with a brilliantly sharp ear
for slips of register and slack words. To both I am immensely
grateful.

Earlier versions of a number of these poems have been
published in various journals: 'Pickpocket Naples 1, and 2',
in *The New Yorker*; 'Flute for the Children', 'Darning Egg
and a Workbox', 'One, Two' , 'Marina' and 'A Lighthouse'
in the *Times Literary Supplement*; 'Livelong Day' in *Poetry
Chicago*; 'Janacek's Notes', 'A Cricket for Pirandello', 'Sage',
'Toccata for the *Pezzentelle*', 'Naples Abstract', 'St Lucy's
Day', 'A Harrowing', 'Tesserae' and 'Swing Song' in *PNR*;
'Barn Owl' in *The London Magazine*; 'Steps for a Sarabande'
in *The Dark Horse*; 'The Mower' in *Spiritus*; 'Island / Poem'
and 'Roses / Remembrance Day' in *The Compass Magazine*;
'Hymn for a Tree' on *www2.mmu.ac.uk/write*; 'A Counting
Song' on *www.trin.cam.ac.uk/news/a-counting-song*. 'A
Cricket for Pirandello' was commissioned for a volume in
honour of the French scholar and translator, Roger Pearson:
Gravity and Grace: Essays for Roger Pearson, ed. Charlie
Louth and Patrick McGuinness, Legenda, MHRA, 2019.

'Brick Wall' was commissioned for a celebration of Roy Fisher, publication postponed until summer 2021. My two translations, one strict, one reflective, of Dante's 'Purgatorio', Canto 10, were commissioned for *Dante, 'Purgatorio': Translations by Contemporary Poets*, ed. Nick Havely with Bernard O'Donoghue, Todmorden: Arc Publications, 2021. In addition, 'Barn Owl', 'Stilt-Jacks', 'Saving his Gloves', 'Humming-Bird Hawk-Moth' and 'Wet Suit' all appeared as a pamphlet: *Clutag Five Poems Series, No 21*, ed. Andrew McNeillie.